Flowerbeds With Headstones

Flowerbeds With Headstones

Cara Cohn

WALNUT STREET
—PUBLISHING—

ISBN 979-8-9893320-6-9

Walnut Street Publishing
1645 S Holtzclaw Ave
Chattanooga, TN 37404

To Mema & Mom
Since the beginning, forever, and always.

my skeletons
didn't keep well
in my closet,
so I tucked them
in my garden.

I do so wonder,
why don't my flowers grow?

did you bury them
or did you lay them to rest, my dear?

1

Baa-Baa Black Sheep

I think about the way
You had to celebrate
Or dread
Alone
Probably in the bathroom
Of a place
You didn't call
Home
Surrounded by
The silence
Of people
That should've
Been there,
I wonder if
Your ring finger felt
Naked
Or if you felt
Prepared,
I wonder often
If you started to cry
Or held your breath
Or laughed
Or screamed
Or puked
Or called someone
When you found out
The news

A black sheep
Of the family
Was going to have
A little black lamb too

Sweet Girl

The soft sound
Of lead
Scratching paper
Was as loud as my voice
Could ever get,
My two eyes
Were the only ones
That listened
To what I wrote,
My stuffed bears
And shooting stars
Were the only things
That knew how I felt,

You say
I miss when you were soft and sweet
But this is not quite
How you remember me.

Blended

In the beginning
I didn't know
How people perceived me
Or what their intention was
With certain vocabulary

"Biological family?"
"Step or half-sibling?"
"Where's your real daddy?"

But soon I learned to dread

"Classmates" and
"Sunday mornings"

And worst of all

"Draw your family tree"

Draw Your Family Tree

I carried 4 names passed to me
Before I reached the age 13
The first I carried from my mother's previous divorce
Born out of wedlock,
With no father to claim me.
My second name from my mother's second marriage
Where we trespassed into victimhood
And left survivors.
My third name came
From a second-hand maiden name
Because my mother herself carried two,
From her half-assed step father who applied
for the position but
couldn't fill the _daddy_ shoes.
My fourth name came
When she tried one last time,
And we finally grew a family tree –
But these are not all the names I carry.
I carry the true maiden name of my mother,
Hernandez
Or that's how it would sound
If I spoke our mother tongue,
Or if my mother spoke her mother tongue,
Or had her father present to teach her in the first place.
I carry my grandmother's own
second-hand maiden name
From yet another over-step-ping father
Because our cycles are long and strong
But the marriages were not.
I carry the family name

6

From Irish predecessors
That wouldn't know what to do with some of us
If they saw our complexion,
I carry my Uncle's Mexican name
And all his beatings that came with it
From the neighborhood kids,
I carry my Cousin's name
And the new one her foster family gave her,
As well as my Sister's married name
From a wedding I never attended,
I carry my Brother's heirloom name
From extended step-family
That didn't love me as much as they talked about me,
And I carry all the names
Of family I don't know
Starting with the first name
Of the man that didn't come
To collect my birth certificate.

I carry these names
Sewn together like a quilt
With holes and ripped patches
Faded colors
And loose stitching

But nevertheless, it keeps me warm.

Mirror Mirror

I festered rage
For far too long
At a world that held
No space for me,
Shelving my personality,
Shrinking my opinions and
Corroding my identity.
Trauma-bonded with my insecurities,
Infected with a victim mentality,
I didn't take any responsibility.

Oh, how well my oppressor's shoes fit me.

Lullaby

There are times
Nowadays
When failure seeps into
The shelter of my sheets
To accompany me
With everyone I feel
I should've made
Happy

So, tell me, do you have any siblings?

I miss the days when I missed you,
because sorrow kept me closer to you
I hate that I still think about you
when it feels like there's no point
I don't know how to talk to you –
I don't even think I like you,
But how would I know? we don't talk.
I hate that if I called you I wouldn't know what to say,
I hate that when we last spoke
you mostly shit-talked [my] mom,
I hate understanding where it came from.
I don't like the anxiety I feel around you
Or your shitty effort to fix things,
And I hate that only part of me wishes you'd stop.
I wish I could hate you the way I used to,
Or that I didn't have to keep up with you because
I feel forced to,
And I hate feeling more comfortable
Surrounded by strangers
Than I do isolated in a room with you.
I hate that if we weren't related
I wouldn't know how to be friends with you
And I dread when therapists or first dates
ask me about you.

I hate that I don't like the way your hugs feel
But I hate it more that I want to ask you for one,
And I hate that I won't,
And one day I'm going to hate that I wish I did.
And I hate the fact that I don't hate you,
And that I'm so broken the only times
I feel like I love you
Are when I could lose you
And that I don't know how to fix this,
Or if I even want to
And the only reason I keep a picture of you
Is to remind me I have an obligation to remember you.

Come Visit Me

Have a seat at my table,
I hold space for you here,
Teach me how to make your coffee
So I can listen to your voice once again,
Grab a mug, hug it close,
And maybe one day we'll do the same.

Let me take a look at your wounds,
Have they healed or
Have they festered?
Did you find what caused them,
And will your remedy work on mine?
Did you smother your infection
Or did you let it breathe?
Are you only able to love others
With the same matching injuries?

One moment,
Let me pour you another cup of coffee.

Does silence make you uncomfortable
Or is it just with me?
The creaks in your chair crinkles the quiet
As you shift in your seat.
Are there parts of you you're hiding
From yourself as well as me?
You don't have to answer,
It's okay if you don't know everything.

You want more sugar?
Here – have the whole jar.

Do you think – maybe,
Would you, perhaps,
Like to be friends?
I know it's an odd concept
But maybe,
Eventually, perhaps,
We can be sisters again?

The bathroom?
It's the last door at the end.

The room feels tense
With your familiar absence.
I release held breath
Trying to return to the present moment.
My mug burns my hands
I've clutched it for far too long
I poured myself another cup,
But I'm not quite sure when.

What's the time?
Wow, it's gone by fast.
Do you have somewhere to go?
That's okay, I understand.

Please, don't apologize for the coffee ring,
It's evidence you were here,
Despite our history.

Identity

and i grasp
and i grasp
and i grasp
at my shell,
at its pieces
till my fingers
blister and bleed
praying i don't fall apart
when my vices
infect my stability,
and i beg
and plead
and pray,
please run from me.
my trauma feels contagious,
i don't think
it healed properly.

Sweet girl,
let go of your trauma-identity.

Giggle

I wonder how your laughs would sound
Woven in the threads of my pillows,
Or if they'd echo through my home
Like windchimes through a porch window.

It's been so long since your soul
Sung your melody,
Do your lungs still know the feeling
Of joy?

My Mother Was A Child First

I sometimes dream of a different life for my mother,
One where only jewelry rests on her neck
And hugs are the only squeezes she knows,
Or knowing bathrooms to just be bathrooms
Instead of places to talk on the phone.
I dream of a life where she can giggle about making love
Over a glass of wine on a girl's night,
Because it's what
she desired.
I wish my mother only knew
To hold her breath going through tunnels
Or that eggshells are just eggshells,
And her car is a means for adventure, not escape.
I wonder of the child my mother would be
If she had papa Bears instead of Grizzlies,
And she didn't have to kiss frogs
To feel like royalty,
Or if she had brothers who were just brothers
Instead of American-family refugees.

I wonder of the mother my mother would be
If I got the chance to shelter her
When she was a child
Instead of thirty years too late,
And I wonder if she knows
I'd raise her again and again in any lifetime
No matter how many childhoods it would cost me.

It takes a village
To raise a child

But it takes a village
To heal one too

Inherent Value

Flowers are still beautiful
Nestled in the ground
As they are a vase,
Just as a song
Still holds a melody
When sung in
An empty room,
And paintings are still
Masterpieces
Without admiration,
And, oh –
how powerful
And bright
Stars would remain
If no more women
Wished upon them
Deliverance into
Something different.

Don't wait up for me
I fell asleep on my garden swing,
I was busy picking flowers
And making my deliveries,
I left bouquets on steps where
Mending was overdue,
And hand-delivered others
With cards that read,
I'm sorry and
I forgive you,
So please don't wait up for me
I'm basking in the sun
On my garden swing,

Resting in peace